# 57 Minutes

## All That Stands Between You And A Better Life

# 57 Minutes

## All That Stands Between You And A Better Life

*Mike Jackson and Pierre Lever*

Copyright © 2011, Mike Jackson and Pierre Lever

ISBN 978-1-105-20907-9

# Contents

What this Book is all About ............................................... 1

Make time Stand Still .......................................................... 3

Use Fear to Your Advantage ............................................. 9

Rethink "Work-think" Part I: Design Your
Dream Job ............................................................................ 15

Rethink "Work-think" Part II: Quit Your Way to
Success .................................................................................. 19

Make a Life List .................................................................. 25

Think Backwards to Get Things Done ........................... 29

Recharge Your Batteries .................................................... 33

Be an Ironman® ................................................................... 39

Gather a Personal Fortune of Experiences .................... 43

Celebrate ............................................................................... 47

Don't Label Anything "Once in a Lifetime" ................. 51

Listen to Your Mother ....................................................... 55

Live Your Life as a Story .................................................. 59

Bringing it all Together ..................................................... 65

Recommended Reading List ............................................ 69

Acknowledgments .............................................................. 71

About the Authors .............................................................. 73

## Dedication

*To Cathy, Lilly and Greg*
*To Sarah, Eleanor, Alice and Kitty*

# What this Book is all About

*"You forget what you hear, you remember what you see, but you learn what you do."*

From the moment you read these words to the moment you finish the concluding paragraph you will have spent less than an hour absorbing a number of powerful ideas that will help you lead a happier life.

We have written this book to provide a *short, effective, and honest* guide to help regular people like us – with jobs, relationships and limited time – make their lives more fulfilling each day.

- It is *short*, because it shouldn't take much longer than about 57 Minutes to read.
- It is *effective*, because it explains clearly what you can do to turn the recommendations into actions.
- It is *honest*, because we have applied all the concepts in our own lives, and seen others do the same in theirs, with amazing results.

Every recommendation in this book is a result of extensive reading, observation and, most of all, personal experience. Where we were inspired by something we have read, we reference the source of inspiration. Where we have observed one of our recommendations in practice, we give you the example. As for personal experience, this lies at the heart of everything we share throughout the pages that follow.

We want this book to transform not just inform.

If you like half the ideas in the book and implement only half of those, that is fine (not great, but fine). A 25 percent return outweighs the 57 Minutes you would have invested.

If you like all the ideas but implement nothing you would probably have been better off spending your 57 Minutes catching a power nap.

The Chinese have an expression, "You forget what you hear, you remember what you see, but you learn what you do." This is a book about doing, and it is packed with recommendations that work. We hope you enjoy putting them into practice as much as we have.

# Make time Stand Still

*"...short term kicks don't lead to long term life improvements."*

In an effort to reach a state of long term happiness, we've found that many people choose to experiment with quick-fix, short term remedies that, more often than not, end up in failure. Indulgence in these short term pleasures (rather than activities that provide much deeper fulfillment) actually turns out to be a significant limiter to real happiness, contrary to what you might have intuitively thought. For us, understanding this phenomenon was the first step to understanding the path to a more fulfilling life.

Dr. Martin Seligman, well-known author and expert in positive psychology, highlights the difference between short term *pleasures* and deeper *gratifications* in his book *Authentic Happiness*. He describes a pleasure as being, "something with clear sensory or emotional components that involve very little, if any, thinking." There are many of these: chocolate, sex, wine, an impulse purchase, relaxing in front of the TV to name but a few. Come home from work, slump on the sofa and turn on the TV. Feeling blue, grab a beer from the fridge. Bad day at the office, get the credit card out for some retail therapy.

The problem is not that these pleasures make you unhappy, or that we consider them bad. Far from it – actually, any combination of pleasures will give you a lift at the very least and, in moderation, they're certainly not about to ruin your life.

So, what is the problem?

The problem is simply that these short term kicks don't lead to long term life improvement. You can easily find yourself in an everlasting pursuit of pleasures. The more pleasures you indulge, the more your expectations rise in tandem and the harder it becomes to gain any real, long term satisfaction. The result is zero permanent gain in your levels of happiness.

A life spent snatching up pleasures is unlikely to give the sort of life improvement we think you should obtain.

Gratifying acts are different.

Gratifying acts are ones in which you so immerse yourself that time seems to stand still. They don't necessarily provide you with an emotional kick. Instead, they're activities that fully engage your mind and revolve around your areas of deepest interest rather than short term desires.

The trick to determining what a gratifying act is for you is to first figure out what the activities are that you can associate with the moments where *time stops*, where you're so fully absorbed in the activity that you lose track of time.

As you can imagine, this list of activities is as unique as there are personalities in the world, and it is rather unlikely that you'll have yours finalized by the time you reach the end of this chapter. Reaching your ultimate level of sustainable happiness is a quest. It starts with first recognizing that the perpetual over-indulgence of pleasures isn't getting you any closer to that end goal of a better life. Uncovering your gratifying acts – those activities that you find most fulfilling – and finding as many ways as possible to assemble your life around them is the most significant step you can take towards measurable and consistent life improvement.

Let me give you examples from my life:

I have an intense curiosity about the world and gain deep satisfaction from new possibilities and fresh ideas. I instinctively gravitate towards situations where judgment and critical thinking are required, and I relish the process of dissecting and solving problems. I can easily lose track of time when given the opportunity to guide and counsel others.

So, how do I use this to structure a happier life?

I build as many activities as possible into my life that somehow touch these characteristics.

- At work: I look for organizations and projects with complex issues to satisfy my desire to solve problems; I seek out opportunities to coach and develop employees; I throw myself at new opportunities in my job and career to keep things fresh and interesting.

- At home: I'm a news junky and read compulsively about life, business, and people to satisfy my thirst for new knowledge; I have also embarked on writing this book as a way to expand my experience in helping others improve their lives.

- At play: I travel extensively to new places so I can keep my horizons broad and my brain wired-in to how the world really works; and I socialize with people with whom I share similar interests to ensure lively discussions about issues facing the world.

All of these activities give me deep, long lasting satisfaction because they're built on the things that make me ... well me, when I'm at my best.

To identify your gratifying acts, we suggest keeping a diary and using it to monitor and measure the underlying reasons for the satisfaction you get from the activities that absorb you most.

Here's how to do it:

- Get a diary and start recording the key activities in which you participate. Be diligent about recording what you do every day for a month. Generally, over the course of a month, you'll encounter most of what gives you deeper satisfaction.

- Give each activity a rating according to how absorbed you were when performing it, one being "completely bored" and five being "fully absorbed." Rate your activities according to the extent to which time stood still. Your friends and family can help; ask them for input on when they noticed you at your least and most absorbed.

- Identify patterns: Combine activities with similar characteristics, and similar ratings, into groups. As you do this, you'll begin to notice patterns – the activities that engage you more than others will also start to show similar characteristics.

- Extract your underlying gratifications: Think long and hard about these patterns and the activities within them. Ask yourself what it is specifically that gives you such satisfaction about the activities within these patterns. Make a list of the answers – these are your underlying gratifications.

- Build your personal database of gratifying acts: Using your list of underlying gratifications, create an expanded list of gratifying acts by thinking about what else is available for you to do (or try) that would also satisfy your list.

With your underlying gratifications identified, and a new and improved list of gratifying acts in-hand, you can start adding these new activities to your daily routine: at work, at home, and at play. We see this as a great first step to life improvement as it helps form the foundation upon which the techniques we'll explain in the coming chapters will build.

## Make Time Stand Still

*Identify absorbing activities that make time stand still when you do them – build as many of these as possible (rather than just short term kicks) into your daily life.*

# Use Fear to Your Advantage

*"Getting the most out of life requires breaking through your fears and accepting that the risk of failure is a far better gamble than the risk of not really having lived at all."*

There will always be things to worry about – something from the past that you wish hadn't happened or a potential risk that you hope won't. These feelings of anxiety are common and perfectly normal. In fact, only a very small percentage of people truly live worry free.

Having the courage to push through your fears and act when action is needed is the key to trying new things, getting things done, and rebounding quickly when things go wrong. Getting the most out of life requires breaking through your fears and accepting that the risk of failure is a far better gamble than the risk of not really having lived at all.

You're significantly more capable of fulfilling your ambitions than you probably think, and very often the only thing in your way is *you*. The concept of self-doubt ruining your plans for bigger things has been documented in many self-help classics for good reason. Self-doubt is a destructive force – a manipulative menace that wrecks your chances for life improvement by digging up all your negative memories and experiences with the only objective of convincing you that it is not possible to reach your goals.

So, if worrying is normal, and we all do it, but living a more fulfilling life requires us to overcome our irrational fears and self-doubt, what should we do?

The first step is to understand when and why you're worrying.

- Become acutely aware of the moments when your fears are getting the better of you – those moments when you've decided to do something exciting and you start to convince yourself not to try. Bring these moments into clear focus and recognize just how detrimental this fear is to your life. Deconstruct the irrational fear and recognize it for what it is: unhelpful, unwanted, and unnecessary.

- Ask yourself, "What is the worst that could happen?" Of course the answer to this may occasionally be serious, but in the vast majority of cases the worst that can happen is usually far less dramatic than the level of anxiety that precedes it. More likely than not, the worst case scenario is a small, temporary failure where you learn something new and probably something about yourself as well. It might have cost you some money or caused you some embarrassment, but unless the risk is death or a crippling injury you'll probably grow more by giving it a shot.

- Recognize that mistakes are inevitable in anything we do and that learning to deal with these mistakes is essential to help us develop. Experience works wonders here, because the more mistakes you make, the more you start to understand that making mistakes isn't all that bad and it actually helps us to grow. Michael Jordan, the legendary Chicago Bulls player, sums it up best, "I've missed more than 9,000 shots in my career. I've lost almost 300 games. Twenty-six times, I've been trusted to take the game winning shot and missed. I've failed over and over and over again in my life. And that is why I succeed."

After you've become well acquainted with your irrational fears, the next step is to restructure the way your fear works by eliminating the wrong fears and cultivating the right fears.

Crippling fears, i.e. the *wrong fears*, are those that confine you to your comfort zone. Their objective, as their name suggests, is to keep you safely within the boundaries of your comfort zone by crippling you with fear. They include fears like: fear of embarrassment, fear of failure, fear of getting hurt, and the fear of the unknown. Motivational fears, i.e. the *right fears*, on the other hand, are those that spur you to action. Things like: fear of regret, fear of missing out, fear of stagnation, and the fear of boredom. These fears, if cultivated effectively, help re-train your mind to encourage taking action. The second step to mastering your fear is, therefore, to confront it head-on by reconditioning your mind to focus on motivational fears and eliminating crippling fears.

The two motivational fears that have helped me most in living a fuller life are:

- The fear of lame excuses: When approached with a new idea, something interesting to try or something I would love to do or say I've done, I imagine myself in the situation of explaining my decision to someone I know and care about. I ask myself whether I would rather explain all the reasons why I didn't try (excuses, if you will), or would I rather talk about the cool thing I am going to do or have already done. The latter always wins.

- The fear of regret: I really don't want to look back on my life and regret not having lived an exciting life or not having followed a dream or not having attempted a new challenge. I would much rather try but fail than not try and regret missing the opportunity. Cultivating a genuine fear of regret may not eliminate regret from your life, but it can be powerful and help lift you to greater heights.

Armed with a repertoire of motivational fears, the final step is to simply move past your crippling fears.

This may, at first, sound challenging, but in reality it is highly likely that you have the capability, the capacity, the energy, and the ideas to achieve life changing ambitions. With this in mind, there is no more effective way to silence your self-doubt than to actually push forward and have a go at achieving your goals.

The very act of taking the first step will work wonders and, with each step you take towards achieving your goals, you will notice that your crippling fears wield less influence. They may still be there nibbling at your confidence; but somehow, in the face of your motivational fears, they'll seem less virile, less destructive. The more, new ventures you embark on, the more you will realize that it was *you* holding you back all along.

## *Use Fear to Your Advantage:*

*Missed opportunities are more painful than occasional mistakes – be conscious of your self-doubt, confront it and take the steps to push through your crippling fears.*

# Rethink "Work-think" Part I: Design Your Dream Job

*"...ask yourself what intrinsic happiness your work gives you."*

Most of us spend the majority of our conscious time either at work or thinking about work. Our professional lives dominate our time, our thoughts, and our activities. So, why is it that so many people still don't find the satisfaction from work that they deserve? What is it about our approach to work that makes us sacrifice our happiness today for some future light at the end of a very long tunnel we call a career?

Without properly framing the way you think about work – your *work-think* as we call it – most people run the risk of being, or at least feeling, trapped by their employer, their paycheck, or both at some point in their career. This doesn't need to be the case for any of us, as long as we spend the time and energy to *rethink our work-think*.

Despite all the available advice to the contrary, it is still true that, for many people, the primary motivation for work is *the money*. Many employers understand this and use financial incentives, golden handcuffs, and deferred bonus schemes to keep you on their payroll indefinitely. The problem is financial rewards alone are rarely sufficient to generate the level of happiness at work that you deserve, nor are they sufficient to motivate you to deliver to the best of your ability on the job.

Of course, money is necessary: mortgages need to be paid, food needs to be purchased, and pensions need to be financed. This is not under dispute. However, the real question is what more can you get from your work beyond fulfilling these basic monetary needs.

In his book entitled *Drive: The Surprising Truth About What Motivates Us*, Dan Pink explains that our intrinsic motivations at work are driven by the opportunity to become an expert in something, to perform with freedom, and to feel like there is some underlying meaning to our existence at work. We agree with him. Furthermore, we believe that the trick to achieving work happiness is to figure out exactly what these intrinsic motivations are for you and to build them into your professional life.

We recommend stripping away factors like money, reputation, and career advancement to zoom-in on what gives you the most satisfaction from work. When we ask people to do this, they often respond with CV-type answers, like: "I want to have an impact," "I enjoy creating success," or "I like interacting with interesting people."

This is a good start but not normally the final answer that we're looking for. To get to the final answer, we need to dig deeper by asking the question, "Why?" over and over until, eventually, we get to the actual work activities that give you the most intrinsic satisfaction.

For example, take the answer, "I want to have an impact at work." The process might sound something like this:

Q: "Why is it that you want to have an impact at work?"

A: *"I want to feel that I contributed to achieving a good result."*

Q: *"Why?"*

A: *"Because I enjoy working with people, analyzing problems and figuring out solutions."*

Q: *"Why?"*

A: *"Because nothing stimulates me more than tackling a problem others haven't solved."*

Q: *"Why?"*

A: *"Well, I suppose, because I just love trying to solve complex issues and puzzles."*

What started as the statement, "I want to have an impact," actually boils down to an individual being completely absorbed by "problem solving." The "impact" they create happens to be a good consequence of their problem solving activities. However, their intrinsic satisfaction actually comes from the process of the problem solving itself.

Getting to this answer usually takes at least three "Whys". Once you get there, you've uncovered a powerful truth about what engages you at work and you can use it to design the job – the career – that gives you unending, intrinsic satisfaction.

Next time you have the opportunity, instead of preparing to ask your boss for an increase in pay, prepare your dream job specification. Ask yourself how you can deepen your knowledge in a subject area you enjoy, or create more time to immerse yourself in your area of expertise, or build a development path towards specialization in your main area of interest. The time spent doing this will pay dividends far beyond any pay increase you could ever expect.

> ### Design Your Dream Job
> *Motivation at work is linked to the activities we get the most intrinsic reward from – identify these using "Three Whys?" and build a career around them.*

# Rethink "Work-think" Part II: Quit Your Way to Success

*"...many of the best plans in life start by quitting."*

So, you've taken our advice from the last chapter: you designed your dream job, you perfected your proposal to your boss, and you created the plan for getting all the intrinsic satisfaction you possibly can out of your work. The big day comes for the meeting with your boss. You make the pitch. It was perfect. Your boss responds with, "Thanks for the feel good session *<insert your name here>*, now I think it's time you get back to work."

Well, you win some, you lose some. It is true that designing your dream job isn't always going to result in the success you hoped it would. However, just because you couldn't redesign your job the way you wanted this time doesn't mean you have to sentence yourself to career prison, trapped by your paycheck, or your industry-specific experience.

It is time to think bigger. Think career, not job. Think intrinsic satisfaction, not paycheck. Think getting the most out of your life, not getting yourself through the week without going crazy.

There is no question that hardwork and dedication are required to achieve big things, but what's more important is being able to determine when you've reached that point of diminishing returns where any additional hardwork and dedication will only serve to take you further and further away from your ultimate success. This is when it is not only okay to quit, but you actually should quit.

The message of this chapter is simple: quitting is not the same as failing.

In many cases, quitting may be the only thing standing between you and a happier life. In his book *The Dip*, Seth Godin explains that, "Winners quit fast, quit often and quit without guilt – until they commit to beating the right challenge for the right reasons." This is great advice, and we've both used it many times to our advantage.

There is no shame in reaching the conclusion that the company you work for does not share the culture that suits your working style. There is no shame in realizing that further toleration of a glass ceiling or your autocratic boss is no longer contributing positively to your future. There is no shame in having the capabilities to design, find, or create your dream job whether it's with your current employer, a new employer, or through your own business venture.

What if you just can't quit? You're trapped. You can't give up the paycheck. Your neighbors will think you failed. You'll never find another job. What will my spouse say?

Here's the thing: you're never really trapped unless you think you are. Being trapped at work is only in your mind. If you feel trapped and can't muster up the courage to quit now, then start well in advance to prepare a proper plan for your resignation.

Here are a few tips to keep you safe from the clutches of being trapped in your job:

- Never lose touch with your market value: Even when you're happy with your employer, your boss and your job, you should still keep your finger on the pulse of the job market. Register to receive regular notices from job market websites. Even apply and interview for a few jobs that meet your criteria. This will help you to understand what is out there, how quickly you can find work in your field, and what the market is willing to pay for your unique set of skills. There are more jobs out there suited to you than you might think. Knowing these details will help reduce your tendency to feel trapped.

- Keep a quitting fund: Again, even when things are going well at work, you should be putting some money aside for the odd occasion where you may need to survive for a few months without pay. With an accessible savings plan holding three to six months' worth of your after-tax salary, you'll never have to feel handcuffed to your paycheck again. Chances are you won't need this money, but having it will help your confidence when it comes to quitting decisions.

- Don't fear being fired: If you've been able to keep current in the job market and build a six-month quitting fund, then it is very easy not to fear being fired. Even if you haven't, the truth is it is difficult to find good people. You know this and your boss knows this. If you perform well, keep up with the workload and maintain a good attitude, the chances are that threats are just that. Don't be held to ransom by your boss or your employer. Life is too short for anyone to have to endure that.

- Create positive options: For many years my positive option was to further my studies. I never had to fear quitting or being fired because, if it did happen, I would just use the opportunity to return to the classroom. After finally taking the chance to further my education, I then immediately created a new positive option – to start my own business. I am now preparing the foundation to make it feasible as well. Always having positive options on tap is an empowering way to avoid feeling trapped at work.

After gaining many experiences with purposeful quitting, we've actually found that many of the best plans in life start by quitting. Quitting should be seen as the start of something new for the future, not the failed end of a phase from the past. Later in the book, we'll discuss the use of *Life Chapters* as a way to structure the phases of your life. Knowing when to quit is an important competency required for embracing a Life Chapter approach to happier living. When it is well-considered, for good reasons, and done in a professional manner, quitting is not the same as failing and should be seen as a show of character in those that are courageous enough to take the decisions that will help them lead a more fulfilling life.

## Quit Your Way to Success

*Quitting is not the same as failing – if additional hard work and dedication will only take you further from your goals, it is not only okay to quit it is time to quit.*

# Make a Life List

*"...reflect on all the things you want to achieve in your life and put them down on paper."*

When I was sixteen years old my father told me a story about a man who wrote a list of all the things he wanted to do in his life. The list included some incredible goals like becoming a medical doctor, flying an airplane, and swimming in every ocean. The story, as my dad told it, ended with this man completing his entire list prior to passing away as a fulfilled and enlightened senior citizen. I don't remember much more about the story or any of the details of the list, but I do remember that it fascinated me enough to start my own "Life List" that very evening.

It goes by many names: a Life List, a Bucket List, a 101 Things to Do Before I Die List, but what you choose to call it really doesn't matter. What matters is that you take the time to actually make the list – that is, reflect on all the things you want to achieve in your life and put them down on paper.

Having a Life List is an essential part of getting the most out of your life, because the list itself actually serves to define what "getting the most out of life" really means to you. Only you can define what that is for you; but one thing's for certain, if it isn't defined, it is much less likely to get done.

It is difficult to explain the impact that putting a goal on paper can have on your life, but nonetheless it is amazing the catalyst effect it has on helping you get things done. A goal committed to paper is a reminder of your commitment to that goal, and once you've achieved the goal and checked it off your list, it is a reminder of the effort, energy, and enjoyment that you received through achieving the target.

We recommend creating a ritual out of your list development and annual review. Review your list at least four times a year, and plan a major revision every New Year's Day where you extract a shorter list of things to achieve in the coming twelve months. Use that shorter list to guide your plans for the year.

Don't be shy about adding new things to your list. There are many great resources, magazines, books, and websites available that you can use to help generate creative ideas about what is achievable in your life. Steal from them with pride; they're a great source of cool things to do.

Don't be shy about deleting things you no longer wish to do either. This list needs to stay current for the rest of your life. Just because you wanted to swing naked by the goal posts of your local football club when you were in school but didn't get the chance, doesn't mean you need to make a plan to do it now so you can check-off an obsolete goal.

Regardless of how you decide to structure it, remember ownership of your Life List is yours and yours alone. You make the rules. The only thing really important about the list is: that it exists, that it is a true reflection of your life desires, and that you review it on a regular basis.

My list started small, random, and included various things, such as:

- See a mountain gorilla in the wild
- Volunteer as a fire-fighter
- Visit Machu Picchu, Peru
- Learn to play the guitar
- Swim with dolphins in the ocean
- Work on a farm
- Eat sushi in Japan…

The more I *lived*, the more I added to the list until eventually I had enough goals on it that I needed to start breaking it down into various categories such as: learn, visit, experience, and see, in order to keep everything organized. Now, many years after the creation of my first list, I am still regularly adding new categories and targets and, every January, I set an objective to check-off at least ten new items in the coming year.

I add and subtract targets from my list freely as my mind changes about the importance of the various goals or activities. I've even deleted entire categories from the list that I now no longer consider as Life List worthy. I've also added entire sections and changed categories so that my list is always completely relevant to my life now.

Today, my list is over ten typed pages with more than fifteen different categories. I have maybe a third of the items checked-off, but I never really worry about that. As long as my list keeps growing, and I keep checking things off, then my Life List will continue to serve its purpose.

Don't take our word for it. Grab a piece a paper and a pencil, or sit down at your computer now and start making your own Life List. You'll be glad you did.

> ## *Make a Life List*
> *If you don't know where you're going then you're unlikely to get there – create a written list of all the experiences and achievements you want in your life and update it regularly.*

# Think Backwards to Get Things Done

*"Inspiring as it may be to dream our big dreams actually achieving them requires execution in small, concrete steps."*

Okay, so now that you've created your Life List, it is time to get started on checking things off.

If you've stretched yourself fully in creating your list, you should have set some pretty bold expectations for yourself. If you have, great! If you haven't, no problem, just keep revisiting your list regularly and work at stretching yourself further with each revision.

You'll get there, but your work won't stop there. Your big objectives, now written down, are a crucial element for making a positive life change but unfortunately that's not enough.

This is because of what we refer to as the *inactivity trap*. All too often we take no action towards our objectives, until suddenly the date of the big milestone approaches, and we realize nothing has happened. It is much too easy to get swept-up into daily life, find convenient excuses, and then pretend we were never really interested in the grand plan we'd set out for ourselves in the first place.

Inspiring as it may be to dream our big dreams actually achieving them requires execution in small, concrete steps. Your big objectives need to be broken down into these steps and then planned backwards from the ultimate achievement to the required first action. Each little increment, step-by-step, adds up to the end result of you reaching your target.

We refer to this process as thinking backwards. It is a tremendously effective way to avoid the inactivity trap and actually lies at the heart of most long term success stories.

Let's take, for example, an item from my Life List, "Climb Kilimanjaro".

Honestly, this isn't a tough objective to achieve, but it definitely requires some detailed thinking backwards. Travel plans need to be made, fitness levels need to be reached, clothing and equipment need to be purchased, etc. – there is a laundry list of things to be done in order to reach the summit.

The thinking backwards process dictates starting at the end and working backwards to the current day. So, the first thing we did was decide on the date we wanted to reach the summit. After a small amount of research, we chose August 24th, 2004 because we wanted to reach the peak of Africa to celebrate my brother's thirtieth birthday.

With our summit date chosen, we started stepping backwards, first deciding on the route we wanted to take, which then dictated the minimum equipment and fitness requirements, which ultimately dictated the intensity of our preparation plan.

Preparation plans are most effective when prepared using a calendar so you can: set time bound goals, prepare for them before they arrive, and acknowledge them when they're achieved. It not only helps facilitate the planning, but it also keeps the level of excitement up as you put forth the effort towards reaching the target.

Stepping back through our preparation plans allowed us to establish all of the milestones and lists required to get ready for the big event. We were able to create: our shopping lists, the budget needed for the purchases, our fitness programs, the milestones we needed to reach to ensure we were fit enough in time for the climb, our travel plans, including the travel agent we'd use, our logistics schedules, and the add-on trip to the neighboring Serengeti and Ngorongoro Crater National Parks.

Using this simple concept is a great way to achieve big goals. By breaking them down into small, easily-reachable increments, the big goals seem less intimidating, and the regular milestone tracking helps keep excitement and motivation sufficiently high to maintain the momentum you need to reach the target.

---

## *Think Backwards to Get Things Done*

*Plan objectives from the end goal backwards – be motivated by the goal but focus on the little increments needed to get there.*

# Recharge Your Batteries

*"...the number of hours in the day is fixed but the quality of energy available to use is not."*

Do you sometimes find that, despite your best intentions, the things you want to do the most don't get done? That you feel you don't have the time for the activities you know would give you the greatest sense of fulfillment? While it is popular to find fault in our busy lives and blame this phenomenon on a lack of time, more often than not, the shortage of time is actually not the obstacle. The real issue is a lack of energy.

Energy is the substance that allows you to be physically prepared, mentally focused, and completely connected to the task at hand. The skillful management of your energy is an integral component of sustainable life improvement simply because the number of hours in the day is fixed, but the quality of energy available to use is not.

Our goal with this chapter is to introduce the concept of effective energy management as a means to achieve your optimal levels of positive energy and, in turn, the confidence needed to perform with both your mental and physical batteries fully charged.

How do you achieve your optimal levels of positive energy?

One word, *balance*.

Managing your energy effectively over the long term requires an artful balance between your physical health and your mental freshness. Missing this balance can have detrimental effects ranging from burn-out, dependency, and regret to stunted personal development, estrangement, and divorce. Getting serious about achieving balance in your life is, therefore, an important step to actually improving it.

To help put you on a path to achieving your optimal energy levels here are a few getting started tips on how to find the right balance in your life.

### - Get Organized, Today

Achieving ultimate balance is pretty tough to do accidentally – it requires planning. Planning with two important objectives: first, to create periods of sprints where you can perform at your very best, because these high performance periods are both energizing and draining simultaneously (i.e. balanced, by definition), and second, to create gaps in your schedule that provide for regular and effective renewal or rejuvenation periods, because no one can be expected to perform at their optimal levels all of the time.

Designing productive moments is a simple method for reaching these two objectives. Determine the periods of time when you are most fresh during the day, when you're thinking at your sharpest, and coming up with great ideas. Design your days around creating more of these moments, separated by breaks, and ensure that these moments coincide with when you need to perform at your best.

Here's an example of how I like to plan my productive moments:

- At the beginning of every week I sit down with a one page print out of my weekly calendar. At the top of the page, as a reminder, I write something special that I want to do for, or with, the family. Then, I segment the week into my periods of sprints and rests and populate the sprint periods with my daily to-do lists to ultimately create my working guidebook for the week. On Friday, before leaving the office, I print out next week's calendar and transfer any unfinished items to start the process over. This methodology ensures I've organized my week into productive moments, and it doubles as weekly closure. I leave the office on Friday having cleared my mind of next week's issues, ready to fully engage in the weekend, and free from my work-related mind clutter.

## - Manage Your Physical Energy

It should not come as a surprise to anyone that being physically healthy is an integral part of life-long balance. Sustaining the energy levels you need to carry out your most fulfilling activities is virtually impossible without, at least, a minimal level of health. Unfortunately, even if we consumed the entire book, we would still not be able to cover the topics of fitness and nutrition sufficiently to do them justice.

Nevertheless, your health is important, and we strongly encourage you to research your current health statistics and the impact your eating habits and exercise choices are having on them. Use this information (and the advice of your doctor, if necessary) to find the right combination of food and exercise to give you the energy needed to perform at your best. Crash programs and crazy diets are normally not the answer, but good common sense eating habits and a sustainable exercise regimen are essential to effective energy management. Be realistic and start small, if necessary, but get started. Just getting started on improving your physical health is a huge step to improving the balance in your life.

### - Recharge Your Mental Batteries

As with physical energy, we also need to balance mental energy expenditure with intermittent renewal or re-charge periods that give our minds the rest and relaxation they need to be ready to perform at their best when called upon next. Here's what we recommend:

- Take time for reflection every day: Understanding your behaviors and attitudes, the way in which you deal with people and situations, and how people react to your behavior is essential to developing personal balance. Whether you prefer to do this first thing in the morning or on your way home from work, creating this time for introspection is one of the most important things you can do to maintain balance. Make it a top priority.

- Take your breaks: You have weekends and vacation allotments for a reason – to rejuvenate your mind, to catch-up on family time, and to pursue your passions outside of work. Just like your body needs rest after exercise, it is important to periodically rest your brain from work. This not only helps keep your ideas fresh, but it also works to keep your stress levels down and your motivation up. Enjoy your weekends, and take your vacation – all of it, every year.

## - Abandon the Deferred Life Plan

A person with good short term balance is off to a great start but could still fall prey to a miserable *deferred life*, living only for that light at the end of the tunnel we mentioned in "Rethink Your Work-think Part I." To avoid this trap, we suggest framing your life into phases, which we cover in more detail in "Live Your Life as a Story." By designing these phases, what we like to refer to as Life Chapters, you create regular opportunities to insert longer term, rebalancing activities into your life.

Here's an example from the long term portion of my own life balance plan:

- Between 1999 and 2005 I was extremely busy with work and was heavily focused on my career. I travelled a lot for business and was in the office for long hours. I was able to maintain a reasonable level of short term balance but, even so, it wasn't sustainable. It was clear that, for the sake of long term balance, an end to this chapter and the start of something new would eventually be required. It was time to recharge and renew my batteries. So, together with my wife, and my brother and his wife, we planned and executed a hundred-day, overland adventure from South Africa to Egypt – an experience we will never forget; the end of one chapter and the start of another.

Finding overall balance for yourself will provide you with significant changes in your levels of sustained, positive energy and your ability to dedicate this energy to the things you truly love. You must make finding balance and managing your energy a priority if you plan to get serious about true life improvement.

## *Recharge Your Batteries*

*Balance is essential for effective energy management – create clear guidelines to ensure your periods of high performance are balanced by opportunities for rejuvenation.*

# Be an Ironman®

*"...the idea of doing an Ironman® is way more difficult than the actual Ironman® itself."*

This chapter isn't actually about doing an Ironman® at all. The real topic of this chapter is something much more life-changing than a really long triathlon. The real topic of this chapter is *the power of thinking big*.

Why use the Ironman® as a place holder for thinking big?

The Ironman® has become known as one of the world's ultimate endurance challenges – 2.4 miles (3.86 km) of swimming, followed by 112 miles (180.25 km) of cycling, followed by a full marathon (26.2 miles, 42.195 km) of running. It's long; it's arduous; and, it's fair to say, rather difficult to complete. If you're good, you can do it in less than twelve hours. If you're great, you can do it in less than ten hours. If you're me, it takes a bit longer.

The truth is an Ironman® is just a triathlon. The only *real* difference is, it's longer.

Actually, there *is* another important difference, a very big important difference:

- The commitment, courage, and audacity it takes for someone to first make that decision to do an Ironman® far exceeds anything it takes to do any regular triathlon.

That is what this chapter is all about.

When I first set out to do my Ironman®, it was pure stubbornness. It had been on my Life List for almost two decades, and I'd made almost no progress towards the achievement. At the time, I wasn't exactly fit, and I had never even done a single regular triathlon in my life (actually, I still haven't). I wasn't getting any younger, and I also wasn't about to fail my list by removing a target as a result of fear – as I said, pure stubbornness. I'm by no means a champion triathlete now, but I did it; I know what it takes, and I can say, without a doubt, the idea of doing an Ironman® is way more difficult than the actual Ironman® itself.

Please don't get me wrong. It was tough, both the training and the event. Triathletes are incredible sportsmen: they're dedicated, they're intense, and they're super fit. They deserve our admiration. The point of this chapter is not to belittle their achievements. The point is only to say that their achievements, and other achievements like them, should not be categorized as super human. That's thinking small.

Being an Ironman® is about thinking big and having the dedication and perseverance to push through the challenges you face to reach your goals. Achieving big things requires big dreams and requires a certain level of physical and mental toughness that we feel is exemplified by the men and women who dare to attempt an Ironman® triathlon, or by those who reach for similar, but equally difficult, dreams of their own.

In "Use Fear to Your Advantage," we successfully conquered the challenge of pushing through your crippling fears. To help you become an Ironman® we now need to tackle the challenge of thinking big.

Thinking big should not be reserved for the Richard Bransons, the Bill Gates, and the Rupert Murdochs of the world. Thinking big is something we could all learn, something we should all practice, and something we would all benefit from. It is a means to reach big heights, not a reward for past success.

Here are some tips to avoid thinking small:

- Don't idolize, instead analyze: Use your admiration of successful people to build a repertoire of successful behaviors. Rather than putting your idols on a pedestal, raise yourself to their level. You can do what they did as well, as long as you start thinking that you can.

- Be creative, not destructive: Brainstorming is a great way to generate ideas. One idea leads to another, and eventually the right one comes up. What makes brainstorming such a successful technique is that no idea is bad, no idea is too big, and no idea is discarded. Brainstorm your ideas with others to build even bigger goals. See who can come up with the biggest.

- Don't blame money, instead budget: Believe it or not, most of the exciting things to do in this world don't require as much money as you might think. If you feel as if a lack of money is stopping you from achieving your goals, don't change your goals and don't be discouraged. Instead, stop accumulating things, start saving in manageable increments, and use your time to research less expensive ways to achieve the same result. They exist. You'll be pleasantly surprised at how affordable achieving your dreams really is.

- Dream big, stay strong: Having big dreams is great, but talking the talk without planning, and taking, your clear path to action is pointless. Have the courage to overcome the hurdles you'll encounter along the way. The journey to a better life is not always reachable on the easy path. Write your goals down, push through your crippling fears and think backwards to create the steps to get there.

Finally, as is true for many of the topics in our book, there are numerous resources available to support you on your quest to thinking big. One book in particular, *The Magic of Thinking Big*, by Dr. David Schwartz, is recommended often in life improvement circles and, although first published many years ago, its advice stands the test of time. We highly recommend reading this book and putting Dr. Schwartz's advice into practice.

Big success is achievable to anyone who wants it enough and can create the opportunity to dedicate the time and energy needed to reach for that success. There is no need to over-estimate the talents of others while underestimating your own. If you want success, you can get there. Start today by thinking big.

## *Be an Ironman®*

*Thinking big is for everyone – be creative, brainstorm big dreams and craft the actions required to exceed them.*

# Gather a Personal Fortune of Experiences

*"For some reason, as we grow older we start to believe that our wealth is a pre-requisite for our happiness – we're wrong."*

If you have ever been around very young children as they're opening presents, you may have noticed that their experience of playing with the wrapping paper often far exceeds the enjoyment they get from the contents of the gift itself.

This is because at a young age the accumulation of physical possessions has no real bearing on happiness. It is the experience of doing or learning something new or different that captivates us. For some reason, however, as we grow older we start to believe that our wealth is a pre-requisite for our happiness – we're wrong.

Although there is, of course, an initial positive sensation from buying something new – a car, a new television, a new watch – this sensation is transient. In the long run, *experiences* are much more satisfying than *things*.

The satisfaction we get from our favorite exercise, a relaxing holiday or a great meal is higher and lasts longer than that which we get from our possessions. With experiences, the satisfaction we feel actually increases progressively together with the experience itself.

Satisfaction from things on the other hand – a purchase of a flash new object for example – peaks for a short period of time and disappears quickly by comparison.

Why?

The best explanation that we've found comes from a study, published in 2010 by Thomas Gilovich and Travis J Carter of Cornell University, where they give three reasons for this phenomenon:

- First, it is very easy to undermine the joy of a new possession through superficial comparisons. If someone bought a nicer, more expensive car than the one you had just bought, it is quite probable that your initial good feeling will dissipate quickly. This is not true with experiences, however. Even if someone went on a more expensive vacation than you, it is very unlikely that the wonderful holiday you just experienced would suddenly seem less satisfying.
- Second, we adapt to new possessions quickly. We get bored with our things easily and our initial burst of happiness ends up not lasting all that long. Experiences are much less vulnerable to this adaptability – we can relive our experiences through pictures and journals, and we can talk about the stories forever.
- Third, possessions just do not engage the mind the way experiences do. Similar to our opening thoughts on true happiness, the comparison between possessions and experiences is like the comparison between pleasures and gratifying

acts. Possessions accumulate and create clutter, whereas experiences accumulate to create knowledge, personal development, great stories, and maybe even expertise.

To quote Professor Dan Gilbert, Professor of Psychology at Harvard University, "...the location of the body is much less important than the location of the mind, and...the former has surprisingly little influence on the latter. The heart goes where the head takes it, and neither cares much about the whereabouts of the feet."

Rolf Potts, independent travel writer and renowned "vagabonder," is an expert in gathering personal experiences through travel. One piece of advice he gives in his book *Vagabonding: An Uncommon Guide to the Art of Long-Term World Travel*, is to develop the knack for "simplification," or the practice of de-cluttering your life by reducing your dependency on material things. He says, "...simplicity, affords you the time to seek renewed meaning in an oft-neglected commodity that can't be bought at any price: life itself."

If you are intent on driving life improvement and increasing your levels of happiness, invest your hard earned resources wisely. Do not just accumulate possessions – gather your own personal fortune of experiences instead. The effects are enduring and the happiness you'll experience by comparison far superior.

## Gather a Personal Fortune of Experiences

*Experiences provide deeper satisfaction than possessions – invest more in pursuing great experiences rather than in accumulating things.*

# Celebrate

*"...there are many events that occur during the week that can be celebrated just as vigorously as the arrival of the weekend."*

It is amazing the motivation people can get from even the smallest of celebrations done at the right time for the right reasons. Unfortunately, most of us tend to focus more on the problems that need solving, the things that need fixing, and the events in the news that are traumatic or frightening. Negative stimuli are so prevalent that we often forget how important it is to see the positive aspects of our lives.

Finding reasons to celebrate is easier than you might think. Start by considering all the things that you accomplish in any given day or week. Consider celebrating your own *small wins* as well as those of friends and family members. The objective is to insert as many shared positive moments as you can into your day.

One of the most obvious and common celebrations around the world, for example, is the arrival of the weekend. There is definitely nothing wrong with celebrating Friday. However, there are many events that occur during the week that can be celebrated just as vigorously as the arrival of the weekend.

We're sure you can come up with many personal reasons to celebrate on your own, but to get you started here are some of our ideas to consider:

- Eating well: A healthy order at a restaurant or not ordering the dessert could easily be cause for celebration. Just be sure not to celebrate it with ice cream.

- Sticking to your budget: Long term financial success takes many small, but frequent decisions about your spending and saving habits. Celebrating a good savings day or an intelligent spending decision is money in the bank.

- Getting some exercise: Making the time to keep fit is definitely worth celebrating. Whenever you prioritize your well-being, you've made a great decision worthy of a small celebration.

- Complimenting a friend: Nothing makes people feel great like an unexpected compliment. Foster the art of making others feel good as cause for feeling good yourself.

- Your children's success: No one knows how to celebrate better than kids. Teach them the lifelong benefits of a positive outlook by celebrating achievements together.

Personal celebrations are important but all too often forgotten. Our busy days consume us, and we focus on what needs to get done without paying respects to the things we've already accomplished. Organize some small celebrations in your personal life and see how it goes. We are quite certain your friends and family members will soon follow your lead.

Taking the lead to organize small celebrations on the job is equally as important as your personal celebrations. Normally, celebrating at work is reserved for the big achievements, but celebrating the small wins is equally as energizing and can often have a much bigger impact on day-to-day motivation and performance.

Obviously, it is important to create work celebrations that are aligned with your company culture and the professional obligations of the work that you do. Regardless, we are of the opinion that most workplaces could stand to include more regular celebrations into the agenda. Consider adding these two activities to your repertoire at work:

- Catch someone doing something right: In the book *The One Minute Manager*, authors Kenneth Blanchard and Spencer Johnson talk about the importance of "catching people doing things right." This is the art of the "mini-celebration" and a very effective way to encourage people to keep working, keep trying, and keep stretching for new heights. It shows people the behavior and performance that you want in a way that makes them feel good and want to deliver the same over and over again.
- Organize "Good News Only (GNO) Meetings": When was the last time you had a business meeting where the majority of the conversation was about successes rather than problems? GNO Meetings have strict rules mandating that all topics, discussions, and

actions need to revolve around good news only. Try it. It is a great way to shock the meeting participants when you declare that today's meeting will be to discuss only the good things that have happened or will happen shortly. Even the biggest naysayer in the group will leave the room smiling or, at a minimum, a bit surprised.

Celebrating the small things in life, whether at home or at the office is a great way to keep a positive outlook – an essential element to improving your overall level of happiness.

## *Celebrate*

*We are so often confronted with negative stimuli that we forget the good things in our lives – find every opportunity you can to celebrate.*

# Don't Label Anything "Once in a Lifetime"

*"There are very few things in life that truly qualify as 'once in a lifetime', don't give this label out arbitrarily."*

You might be wondering why a book about dreaming big, setting stretch goals, and taking action to get things done would have a chapter dispelling the myth of the existence of once in a lifetime experiences. We admit it is a rather peculiar title, but with the examples to follow we plan to explain just how destructive the careless use of this "once in a lifetime" label can be.

While it may be true that each and every moment we live is a unique event, the truth is that there are very few experiences that really deserve the label "once in a lifetime". Granted, there are a number of events, like the birth of your first child or your high school graduation, that do occur only once in life, but the reality is that labeling even these special events as "once in a lifetime" is dangerous and creates unnecessary risks to your enjoyment of the experience.

Why?

Our lives, and everything in our lives, are a work in progress and each unique experience or event forms part of the journey we're taking through this world. The "once in a lifetime" label is dangerous when handed out arbitrarily, because it completely alters the way we think, behave, and make decisions in relation to events and experiences of such magnitude.

Take the following example for instance:
- A Canadian friend of mine wanted to go on a ski vacation to the Austrian Alps. His wife had always wanted to see the pyramids in Egypt. So, together they started to plan a "once in a lifetime" trip. They decided a stop in Paris would be a great idea, given that they would be in Europe anyway. Then, they added Venice and Rome because they had always wanted to see Italy. Eventually, their "once in a lifetime" trip became so huge it would require too much time off work, too much money, and too much planning. They called it off and instead decided to wait until everything was just right.

That's one small example of how the "once in a lifetime" label can cause problems even getting something off the ground. However, consider what might happen if they did decide to go. Despite the vacation time required, the money they'd need to spend, and the planning burden, let's assume they decided it was worth it. When else would they get this once in a lifetime opportunity? The trip is a go, but the label and the over-inflated expectations now risk destroying the very experience they've been dreaming of their whole life.

Here's the thing: virtually none of the really interesting things available to do, learn, or experience in this life are out of reach for any of us. Everything we set out to do in life is a function of the balance we strike between the various priorities we set for ourselves. We make those decisions. We balance the priorities. We manage the process. We can't, however, always control the outcome.

The real danger of using the "once in a lifetime" label, therefore, is that you separate the particular event or experience from reality by exaggerating its importance and creating unnecessary pressure for perfection. Whether that's perfection in planning or perfection in execution doesn't really matter. The potential spoiled outcome is still the risk.

As you set out to live the most fulfilling life that you can, here are a few tips to help manage the potential disappointments you might face from over-inflated expectations,

- Don't expect perfection: We're not saying don't *strive* for perfection, we're just saying don't make it the pre-requisite for satisfaction every time you embark on a new adventure. Everything is a work in progress, even your life improvement plans. Setbacks will happen. If it won't matter ten years from now, you should ask yourself whether it really matters today as well.
- Make the most of every opportunity: The weather won't always be beautiful, the food won't always be delicious, and the service won't always be exceptional. We're not necessarily saying don't complain, or don't get what you paid for. We are just saying that your attitude will shape the outcome.
- Try again: Just because you've had the opportunity for an amazing experience once, doesn't mean you can't have that chance

again. Just because something didn't go the way you hoped it would the first time, doesn't mean the opportunity is lost forever. There is always a way to re-create any experience. Just give it a go, again.

There are very few things in life that truly qualify as "once in a lifetime", don't give this label out arbitrarily. We suggest avoiding it altogether.

### Don't Label Anything "Once in a Lifetime"
*When you label something "once in a lifetime" you create unreasonable expectations – make the best of every opportunity and, if necessary, try again.*

# Listen to Your Mother

*"…being you is far less stressful than trying to be someone you're not."*

The world is a complicated place. It would be extremely helpful if it came with a user manual or a road map. Oddly enough, and although you probably didn't think it at the time, one of the best road maps to navigating your life was given to you by your mother when she said, "just be yourself."

It is an often used expression, but what does it actually mean?

We believe that *just being yourself* is all about being sincere – being genuine – ultimately being the best *you* that you can be.

It starts with an understanding that, even the most successful and talented people in the world have fears: they worry about things, they second guess themselves, and they wonder whether they made the right decisions. No one is without some form of doubt. Recognizing this doubt as normal is the first step to exposing your true self, because this recognition essentially gives you the permission to put yourself out there with a 'what you see is what you get' approach to the world.

Many people have the tendency to over-inflate other people's confidence levels and underestimate their own abilities. Those who are able to see things as they are, while being true to themselves, are those who end up not only appearing confident but actually feeling confident – and being genuine – at the same time. They reach a point where recognizing that doubt is normal, and resisting the tendency for others' perceived confidence to shake their resolve comes naturally.

This doesn't happen overnight. Being you opens up the channels for self-development through feedback and improved self-awareness. It also demands rigorous self-reflection in the face of (sometimes) quite harsh criticism. Although this can be challenging, the growth curve it creates for your development is exponential. Armed with this new learning about yourself, you become much more comfortable with who you really are. As you expose your true personality to the world, you eventually find that being you is far less stressful than trying to be someone you're not.

Here are some tips to help you start:

- Say what you're going to do and do what you say: Having the courage to make commitments and delivering on them is empowering. Try it. Make some promises and then keep them, no matter how difficult it may feel to do. You'll see just how gratifying it can be.
- Don't be shy about asking for advice: Genuine people ask for advice and are not too proud, or afraid, to take it – when the advice is good, that is. People love to give advice. Ask for it from people whom you trust, and genuinely consider it, but make your own decision on how you feel you should proceed.

- Be humble: Nothing exudes confidence more than a person who is humble. Humility is a rare trait, yet it remains one of the most memorable characteristics of those people who care enough to show it. If you're successful, chances are the people around you already know that; you don't need to remind them. You'll make a much more profound positive impression on them with humility than by bragging about your achievements.

- Fully engage yourself in the moment: My old rugby team used to have a saying, "Go hard or go home." It means, if you aren't going to participate fully in what is important now, then it would be better if you just weren't here at all. No matter how difficult the challenge, or how irrelevant it may be to you personally, there is no better way to expose your true self than by fully engaging in what you're doing right now.

- Build strong relationships: The path to a better life is not a solo trip. You'll need help and you'll need to make time to help others as well. Don't sacrifice your relationships; having people you care about to share successes with makes them that much more worthy of celebration.

- Make others feel good: Empathy for others and genuinely showing respect for the people around you is a wonderful way to demonstrate your sincerity. Say, "please," when you should; say, "thank you," more than you think is necessary, and pay genuine compliments to your friends, your colleagues, and your family. Making others feel good is uplifting and quite simply, the benefits far outweigh the costs.

Becoming the best *you* that you can be requires a full commitment to remaining genuine. There is little point in forging ahead with positive life changes if you end up leaving the *real* you – and the relationships and bonds you have formed – for dust. By adopting a 'what you see is what you get' approach, you create the opportunity for continuous self-development while still feeling completely comfortable with who you really are. Nothing is more stress-free than that.

### Listen to Your Mother

*The pursuit of happiness means becoming a better, more genuine you, not a better someone else – put yourself out there. You'll be glad you did.*

# Live Your Life as a Story

*"When we come across someone with twenty years of experience we ask, 'Is this twenty years of good experience, or just one year of experience repeated twenty times?'"*

There are many people in the world living the same year over-and-over again, repeating the routines that helped them reach the comfort zones they experience today. This is a concept we call *chapter-less living*, the monotonous, life-long repetition of the same experiences over-and-over. It's not good.

How many interesting novels have you read in which every chapter was the same as the previous one except that the central characters become slightly better at what they do slowly but surely over time? That sounds pretty boring doesn't it? Why would anyone want to lead their life that way? Unless, of course, they believed that great experiences, adventure, and diversity are for a chosen few. Well, we do not.

We believe that your life should be lived like a book with each new chapter contributing a fresh new experience to the plot– not a virtual repetition of the chapter before. Growing old is not the same as gaining experience. While everybody ages day-by-day, not everyone packs experiences into their lives at the same rate or with the same quality. When we come across someone with twenty years of experience we ask, "Is this twenty years of good experience, or just one year of experience repeated twenty times?". The answers are often sad and shocking.

What we recommend, to avoid this trap of repeating the same year over-and-over again, is to proactively and deliberately create segments, chapters if you will, into your life as if you were the main character in a book about your life.

Before we tackle how to proactively create the upcoming chapters in your life, it is a good idea to take a look at your life so far and retroactively rationalize the life phases you've already experienced. This is an important exercise, because it helps first to illustrate how creating chapters is quite natural, and second to build a foundation for the future chapters to come.

Please take a moment to think about your past and the major transition periods that you've already experienced in your relationships, your education and your career for example. Chances are, as you've lived, chapters have formed in your life. They may be a bit fuzzy, but more likely than not, they're there. Simply progressing through childhood, adolescence, and adulthood can be considered Life Chapters. They're weak Life Chapters but Life Chapters nonetheless.

If I look back over my career Life Chapters, I can see very specific and distinguishable phases: four years of "Foundation Building" in operations, followed by a chapter I call "Gaining Exposure" where I broadened my horizons and started gaining international experience; then came two different chapters of "Management

Development," separated by a short, eighteen-month chapter I call "Personal Development" and so on and so forth. Each of these phases is categorized according to specific characteristics that define the priorities of that phase. As the priorities start (or need) to change, so do the phases; and it becomes necessary to make a more substantial life change, i.e. move on to the next chapter.

Some chapter transitions I initiated deliberately by my own volition. These are the chapters where it was clear what I needed to do long in advance and I was able to proactively structure the chapters, focus on the defined priorities and prepare for the next transition without too much internal conflict or external interference.

Some chapters were created by chance, where an opportunity appeared that would fit the characteristics of my next chapter earlier than I expected. Here's the thing: if I hadn't proactively designed my future chapters, I would not have been prepared to make what appeared like a very spontaneous decision so easily, with the confidence that it was the right move to make.

So, here's what we recommend in order to start living your life like a book:

- Be Proactive: Spend the time to think about the past phases in your life. Determine where chapters were created naturally and where you could have done something differently to create a new chapter. Use this information, together with your Life List, to design the characteristics of future chapters for your life. Then, proactively seek out changes you can make to help build your chapters. The chance of a perfect opportunity suddenly presenting itself without you looking for it is very small. Perfect opportunities are usually lurking in the dark somewhere waiting for you to make a conscious effort to shine a light on them. It requires effort to find them and a strong commitment to make them happen.

- Be Deliberate: Don't repeat the same year twenty times. Ensure your chapters are substantially different to create growth but sufficiently similar to maintain the stability of your life's foundation. A life spent flitting from one opportunity to the next in the hope that you might stumble on the one that really makes you happy is likely to prove dissatisfying and possibly harmful. Stuff your life story with phases that flow from one to the next in a way you feel comfortable with – without creating repetition: be deliberate about what you want out of each chapter, be deliberate about making each chapter new and different, and be deliberate about your decisions to change chapters.

- Be Flexible: As you define your chapters, proactively seek new experiences, and deliberately ensure sufficient changes from one chapter to the next an overwhelming sea of opportunities will open in front of you. Be ready to make changes that suit your plans even when something doesn't exactly fit. Be sure not to over-estimate the risk of change when comparing it to the risk of monotony. Most importantly, ignore life's sunk costs.

A sunk cost is a cost that has already been incurred and cannot be recovered but, most importantly, should be disregarded for future decision making. Consider a career in which you've invested your time and money but that you don't enjoy. Your investment to-date is a sunk cost and should be ignored. You can have a whole career you don't enjoy or half a career you don't enjoy with the possibility of half a career that you do. Which seems better?

The quality and variety of experiences you put into your story will play a significant role in your long term life fulfillment. Take every opportunity to make it an irresistible read.

> ## Live Your Life as a Story
> *Proactively fill your life with chapter after chapter of amazing life experiences – each one deliberately different from the last.*

# Bringing it all Together

Our goal in writing this book was to share simple, powerful suggestions that we know will improve the quality of life for anyone putting them into practice.

We hope you found the ideas compelling. They are built on solid common sense, observation, extensive reading, and, most importantly, the personal experience of using these and seeing others do the same – with amazing results.

Even though this book should have taken you about 57 Minutes to read, it is *still* likely that several of the ideas have escaped you. That's fine. This is not an exercise in memory. The concepts are just as effective even if you dip in and dip out on an occasional basis.

The real difference will come as you implement the recommendations.

So, let's recap the key ones. Here is the *57 Minutes* cheat sheet:

**Make Time Stand Still:** *Identify absorbing activities that make time stand still when you do them – build as many of these as possible (rather than just short term kicks) into your daily life.*

**Use Fear to Your Advantage:** *Missed opportunities are more painful than occasional mistakes – be conscious of your self-doubt, confront it and take the steps to push through your crippling fears.*

***Design Your Dream Job:*** *Motivation at work is linked to the activities we get the most intrinsic reward from – identify these using "3 Whys?" and build a career around them.*

***Quit Your Way to Success:*** *Quitting is not the same as failing – if additional hard work and dedication will only take you further from your goals, it is not only OK to quit, it is time to quit.*

***Make a Life List:*** *If you don't know where you're going, then you're unlikely to get there – create a written list of all the experiences and achievements you want in your life and update it regularly.*

***Think Backwards to Get Things Done:*** *Plan objectives from the end goal backwards – be motivated by the goal but focus on the little increments needed to get there.*

***Recharge Your Batteries:*** *Balance is essential for effective energy management – create clear guidelines to ensure your periods of high performance are balanced by opportunities for rejuvenation.*

***Be an Ironman©:*** *Thinking big is for everyone – be creative, brainstorm big dreams, and craft the actions required to exceed them.*

***Gather a Personal Fortune of Experiences:*** *Experiences provide deeper satisfaction than possessions – invest more in pursuing great experiences rather than in accumulating things.*

***Celebrate:*** *We are so often confronted with negative stimuli that we forget the good things in our lives – find every opportunity you can to celebrate.*

***Don't Label Anything "Once in a Lifetime":*** *When you label something "once in a lifetime" you create unreasonable expectations – make the best of every opportunity and, if necessary, try again.*

***Listen to Your Mother:*** *The pursuit of happiness means becoming a better, more genuine you, not a better someone else – put yourself out there; you'll be glad you did.*

***Live Your Life as a Story:*** *Proactively fill your life with chapter after chapter of amazing life experiences – each one deliberately different from the last.*

# Recommended Reading List

There is no such thing as a complete life improvement book. In fact, the two concepts don't really go together at all. As you embark on your pursuit of life improvement, remember that there are many resources at your disposal.

Throughout our book, we've mentioned many authors who've inspired us to reach for further heights in our quest for more fulfilling lives.

If you're serious about continuous life improvement, we suggest reading some or all of the following books:

*Authentic Happiness,* Dr. Martin Seligman

*Drive: The Surprising Truth About What Motivates Us,* Dan Pink

*The Dip,* Seth Godin

*The Power of Full Engagement,* Jim Loehr and Tony Schwarz

*The 4-Hour Work Week,* Timothy Ferriss

*The Magic of Thinking Big,* Dr. David Schwartz

*Vagabonding: An Uncommon Guide to the Art of Long-Term World Travel,* Rolf Potts

*The One Minute Manager,* Kenneth Blanchard and Spencer Johnson

*The Monk Who Sold His Ferrari,* Robin Sharma

*Taming Your Gremlins,* Rick Carson

# Acknowledgments

Mike: I would like to thank my incredible wife, Cathy, whose love, dedication, and enthusiasm for life never waver. She has given so much to our joint pursuit of life fulfillment that the debt of gratitude I owe her extends beyond words. To our wonderful kids, Lilly and Greg, who've shown me that re-experiencing life through our children opens-up a whole new series of fantastic adventures. To my brother, Matt, who is never short of a great idea and is always ready to try something cool. To my parents, Larry and Sue, who through their love and guidance taught me that life is something to be lived to its fullest, not observed from the sidelines.

Pierre: I would like to thank my amazing wife, Sarah, who is an inspiration to me every day and one of the most supportive, fun loving, and adventurous people I know. To my beautiful daughters, Eleanor, Alice and Kitty, who create joy out of the smallest things and can snap me out of a grouch in the blink of an eye. To my brother, Antoine, who sees the positive in everything and whose sense of fun is infectious. To my loving parents, Allen and Annick, who taught me kindness, reason, and the importance of family.

Mike and Pierre would also like to thank the people who helped in reviewing and proof-reading the contents of *57 Minutes*. A big thanks to Amanda Skopec, Cathy Jackson, Daniel Huber, James Ireson, John Dodsworth, Jo

Miller, Larry Jackson, Martin Bromfield, Matt Jackson, Tim Robson, Tom Bausemer, Sarah Lever and Sue Jackson. Your feedback and suggestions were very much appreciated and helped us create a far better final product.

# About the Authors

Mike and Pierre met at business school in Lausanne, Switzerland. They formed a firm friendship and, along the way, discovered a common interest in uncovering the secrets of life fulfillment. During a (badly played) round of golf one sunny Saturday in London they hit on the idea of writing *57 Minutes* – a book that would summarize their experiences and ideas about life into a short, easy to read guide for the busy individual.

A sports enthusiast and adventure traveler, Mike has spent his life in pursuit of as many new experiences as possible. With a career spanning multiple industries and international leadership roles, he is currently working on a series of entrepreneurial projects and planning his next "around-the-world" adventure with his wife Cathy and their two children.

Pierre is an avid student of human behavior. Throughout his diverse career as a lawyer, entrepreneur, and business leader he has subscribed to the view that to live is to learn. Pierre is CEO of a research business based in Asia and lives in Singapore with his wife, Sarah, and their three children.

Printed in Great Britain
by Amazon.co.uk, Ltd.,
Marston Gate.